Kennedy

TRAVELING
ON LAND

DEBORAH CHANCELLOR

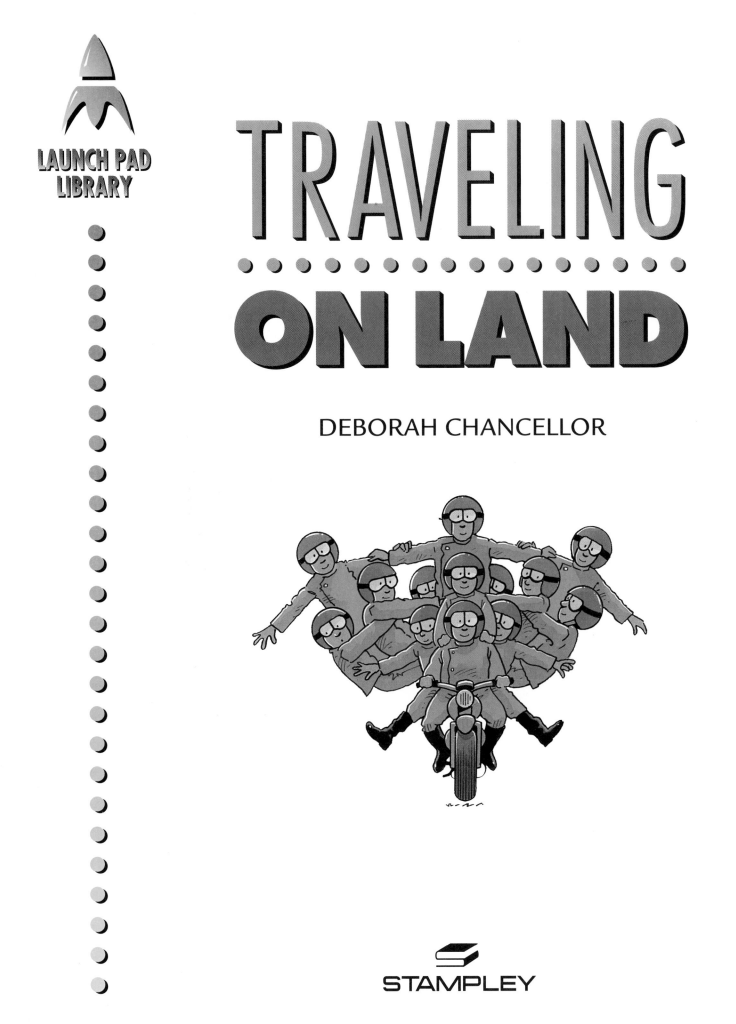

STAMPLEY

How to use this book

Cross-references
Above some of the chapter titles, you will find a list of other chapters in the book that are related to the topic. Turn to these pages to find out more about each subject.

See for yourself
See-for-yourself bubbles give you the chance to test out some of the ideas in this book. They explain what you will need and what you have to do to see if an idea really works.

Quiz corner
In the quiz corner, you will find a list of questions. The answers to the quiz questions are somewhere in the same chapter. Try to answer all the questions about each topic.

Chatterboxes
Chatterboxes give you interesting facts about other things that are related to the subject.

Glossary
Difficult words are explained in the glossary on page 31. These words are in **bold** type in the book. Look them up in the glossary to find out what they mean.

Index
The index is on page 32. It is a list of important words mentioned in the book, with page numbers next to the entries. If you want to read about a subject, look it up in the index, then turn to the page number given.

Contents

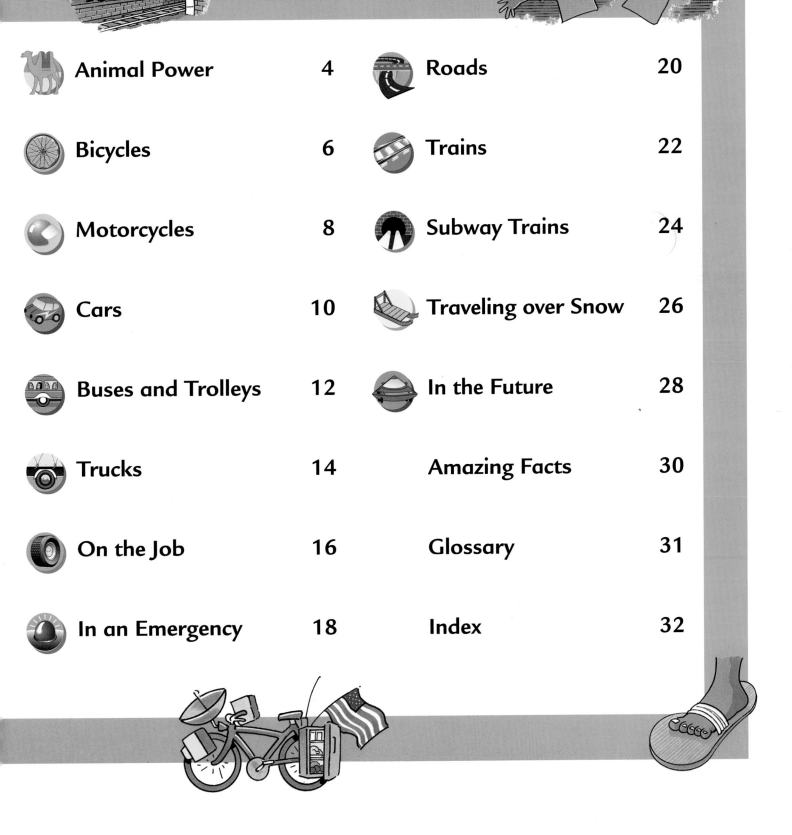

Animal Power

Thousands of years ago, the only way people traveled was by walking. Then they learned to ride animals from one place to another. Traveling became much easier when an ancient people, called the Sumerians, invented the wheel. Animals could then pull carts carrying people and loads. Today, animals still help people travel and do their work.

Inventing the wheel

The first wheels were made of solid wood. They were strong but heavy, and turned slowly. Over time, half-solid wheels were made. These were lighter and turned more easily. Wheels with **spokes**, the lightest wheels of all, are as strong as solid ones.

Taming animals

Most animals must be tamed and trained before being taught to carry loads or people. An animal that pulls a cart learns to wear a harness that attaches to the cart.

▼ Llamas have cloven, or split, hooves, which help them grip as they travel along mountain paths.

▲ These horses are pulling a stagecoach full of passengers and their baggage.

Working animals

In many parts of the world, animals are used to do work that people find difficult. Some animals, such as elephants, can move loads that are too heavy for people to carry. Other animals, such as llamas and camels, are useful because they can travel to places that cars and trucks cannot reach.

▲ Elephants in Thailand have been trained to move heavy logs with their trunks.

look at: Motorcycles, page 8

Bicycles

A bicycle is a simple machine that has two wheels. You make it move by turning the pedals with your feet. A bicycle is cheap to run and does not **pollute** the air. This is because it has no **engine**. All around the world, adults and children ride bicycles, especially in places where cars cannot go.

Changing to a low **gear** *makes it easier for the rider to pedal uphill.*

The handlebars let the rider steer and balance the bike.

▲ This cyclist is stunt riding. He is wearing padded clothing, a helmet and safety goggles to protect him if he falls off.

The brakes rub against the wheel to slow down the bike.

An American named Steve Roberts has invented the world's strangest bicycle. It has four computers and a refrigerator on board, which are all powered by the sun's rays.

*The chain carries **power** to the back wheel and makes the wheel turn.*

*Tires grip the road better because they have a rough pattern on them called **tread**.*

The pedals are linked to the back wheel by the chain.

Bikes for hire

In some countries, people use pedicabs to travel around town. These are similar to bicycles but usually have three wheels. People pay the pedicab operator to take them to where they want to go.

▲ Often, it is quicker and cheaper to travel by pedicab than by car or taxi.

Quiz Corner

- Do bicycles pollute the air?
- What does a bicycle chain do?
- Which part of a bicycle lets you steer and helps you balance?
- What is the pattern on a tire called?

look at: Bicycles, page 6

Motorcycles

A motorcycle is similar to a bicycle, but it is powered by a gasoline **engine**. It is also stronger than a bicycle and can travel faster. In 1885, the first motorcycle was built in Germany by Gottlieb Daimler. It could travel at about eight miles per hour. Today, motorcycles can reach much higher speeds. The world record is 322.87 miles per hour.

CHATTERBOX

How many people do you think can balance on one motorcycle? In 1987 in New South Wales, Australia, 47 people managed to ride on a single bike.

A biker must wear a helmet to protect his head in case of an accident. ....

A shield made of tough, clear plastic protects the biker from the wind. ....

A biker wears strong leather clothing to protect his body and keep him warm. ....

Gripping the ground

As a motorcycle moves along, rough **tread** on the tire causes **friction** between the tire and the ground. Friction helps the tire to grip the ground.

▼ The tires on trail bikes have an especially deep tread to help them grip rough, wet and muddy ground.

SEE FOR YOURSELF

Glue a kitchen scouring pad to one side of a block of wood. Slide the block of wood down a slope, first with the smooth side down and then with the scouring pad side down. The side with the scouring pad makes more friction, so it takes longer to slide down the slope.

Trail bikes

Not all motorcycles are built to be ridden on roads. A trail bike can travel across rough country, even in places where there are no dirt tracks. It can also climb hills and cross streams.

Tread on the tires gives more grip on wet roads.

Quiz Corner

● Who built the first motorcycle?

● Why do motorcycle tires have tread?

● What kind of a motorcycle can climb hills and cross streams?

look at: Roads, page 20; In the Future, page 28

Cars

One of the easiest and quickest ways to travel is by car. Like motorcycles, most cars have gasoline **engines**. Inside the engine, gasoline burns to make **energy**, which turns the wheels. The first car with a gasoline engine was built in 1885 by a German named Karl Benz. It had three wheels and moved very slowly.

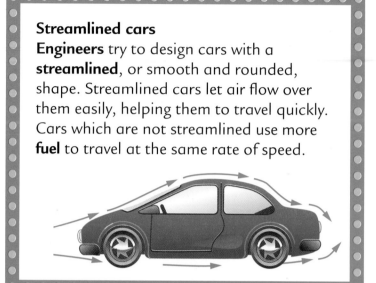

Streamlined cars
Engineers try to design cars with a **streamlined**, or smooth and rounded, shape. Streamlined cars let air flow over them easily, helping them to travel quickly. Cars which are not streamlined use more **fuel** to travel at the same rate of speed.

In most cars, the engine is at the front of the car, under the hood.

At night, drivers use headlights to see the road ahead. Turn signals at the side of the car show when it is about to turn left or right.

Drivers use the steering wheel to turn the car.

Seat belts help protect drivers and passengers if they are in an accident.

NY 3710

Designed for speed

A race car has a very streamlined shape to help it travel at high speeds. The driver sits strapped into a snug seat.

◀ During a race, mechanics work quickly to change the car's tires and fill it up with fuel.

Busy roads

Today, there are more cars on the road than ever before. In cities around the world, such as Mexico City, Mexico, there are sometimes so many cars on the road, that nobody can move. This is called gridlock.

At night, tail lights make the car visible from behind.

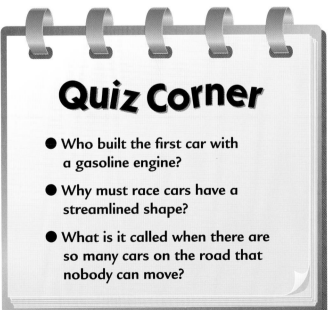

Quiz Corner

● Who built the first car with a gasoline engine?

● Why must race cars have a streamlined shape?

● What is it called when there are so many cars on the road that nobody can move?

look at: Cars, page 10; Trains, page 22; In the Future, page 28

Buses and Trolleys

If more people traveled by bus instead of by car, there would be less traffic on the roads. Buses carry lots of people at one time. They are good for short trips around town and for traveling long distances. One bus uses less **fuel** than if all the people on board traveled in their own cars.

Public transportation

Most cities have a group of buses that people pay to use. This is one type of public transportation. Each bus follows a different **route**, usually marked by a different number. People wait for the bus along the route at bus stops. When people get on the bus, they pay for their trip.

▼ This bus is on a route through London, England. It has two **decks** and can carry about ninety people.

15 Canning Town Poplar
Aldgate St Pauls
Aldwych Trafalgar Sq

CANNING TOWN

EAST LONDON

TOWER BRIDGE

RML 2456

JJD 456D

Long-distance travel

Some large buses, called coaches, travel long distances, from one city to another. They are designed to make journeys as pleasant as possible. They have toilets and soft seats, and sometimes they even show videos on board.

Quiz Corner

- Name a type of public transportation.

- How do some trolleys pick up electricity?

- Where could you catch a ride on the world's longest bus route?

- Why are trolleys a good type of public transportation?

◀ Around the world, many buses are decorated and brightly painted. They can be very crowded.

Trolleys

In some cities there are trolleys as well as buses. Trolleys run along steel rails that are sunk into the road. They are a good type of public transportation because they cause very little **pollution**.

How trolleys work

Trolleys are powered by electricity. Some trolleys are run by a frame on the roof, called a pantograph, which picks up electricity from cables running high above the street.

pantograph

cables

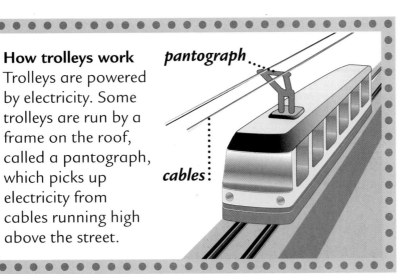

CHATTERBOX

The world's longest bus route is in South America, between Buenos Aires, Argentina and Caracas, Venezuela. It is 6,003 miles long and takes about nine days, including stops.

Caracas

Buenos Aires

look at: On the Job, page 16

Trucks

A truck is a large **vehicle** that carries **freight** from one place to another by road. It is often the cheapest way to transport heavy loads. Different types of trucks carry different kinds of loads. Refrigerator trucks carry fresh or frozen foods. Inside, they have special equipment to keep the food cold.

A powerful engine

A truck needs a powerful **engine** to carry its heavy load. A special hood over the cab, called an air deflector, makes the truck more **streamlined**. This means that it uses less **fuel**. Most trucks run on a special fuel called **diesel**.

▼ Before the driver begins a journey, mechanics make sure that the engine and wheels are working properly.

Tractor trailers

A tractor trailer has two parts. At the front is a cab, or tractor, and at the back is a long trailer. The two parts are joined by a hinge, which lets the driver's cab turn before the trailer.

air deflector

trailer

cab

▲ A tanker, one kind of freight truck, is specially built to carry liquids, such as oil. The tanks are tightly sealed so that they do not spill their load.

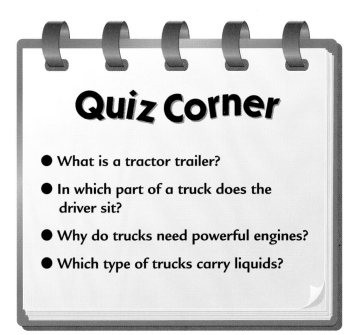

Quiz Corner

- What is a tractor trailer?
- In which part of a truck does the driver sit?
- Why do trucks need powerful engines?
- Which type of trucks carry liquids?

▼ A car carrier is a long freight truck with two or more **decks**. It can carry many cars at one time.

Trailers

Trucks with two trailers are called doubles, and those with three trailers are called triples. Each trailer in a double or triple is a pup. The inside of each trailer is divided into separate sections to make accidental spills less damaging.

Driving in style

Every year, a truck driver may drive thousands of miles, so the cab of the truck needs to be as comfortable as possible. Behind the driver's seat, there is often a bed with a curtain around it, where the driver can take a rest when he needs to.

look at: Trucks, page 14

On the Job

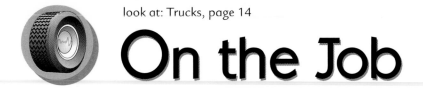

There are many other types of trucks and tractors, and they all do different jobs. Garbage trucks carry trash away from people's houses. Front-end loaders clear soil from the ground. In many places people, including builders and farmers, use heavy equipment to make their jobs easier.

A crane has an arm and hook for lifting heavy loads.

CHATTERBOX

The largest tires in the world are built for giant dump trucks. The tires are twelve feet high, which is about three times the height of a young child.

A bulldozer has a large blade for pushing huge amounts of soil and stones.

The drum of a cement mixer spins around, mixing sand, cement and water to make concrete.

On a construction site Construction sites are full of trucks and tractors. They are used to knock down old buildings, move piles of rubble and even mix cement. Many of the tractors have belted tires for moving on rough ground.

A dump truck takes the soil to a different place. The bed on a dump truck can tip up to make the soil slide out.

16

On the farm

In the past, people or animals did all the heavy work on farms. Today, equipment such as tractors and combine harvesters are used instead. These machines work much faster than people or animals.

◀ A combine harvester does the work of many people. It cuts long lines of wheat and then separates the stalks from the grains.

A front-end loader has a bucket on a long arm that can bend to scoop up soil. It loads the soil onto a dump truck.

Quiz Corner

● The largest tires in the world are made for what vehicle?

● How does a front-end loader scoop up soil from the ground?

● Why do many farmers use machinery to help them with their work?

● What does a combine harvester do?

look at: Cars, page 10; On the Job, page 16

In an Emergency

When there is an emergency such as an accident or a fire, special cars and trucks arrive to help. They must travel to the scene of the emergency as quickly as they can. These **vehicles** are all specially designed to do different jobs.

Fire engines

A fire engine is used to put out fires and rescue people trapped in buildings. It is packed with equipment such as hoses, ladders, buckets and sand. Some fire engines carry huge amounts of water.

▶ Sometimes, firefighters use long ladders to rescue pets that are stuck up high in tall trees.

A long ladder on the fire engine .... can reach to the tops of tall trees or buildings.

Firefighters must .... wear special clothes and hard hats to protect themselves from injury.

▲ A police car uses loud **sirens** and flashing lights to warn other drivers to keep out of its way when it is speeding along.

18

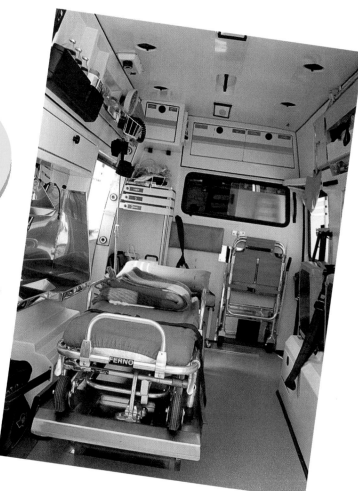

Inside an ambulance

An ambulance is like a small hospital on wheels. Inside, it has life-saving equipment and medicines. It also has a crew of specially trained people. They carry sick people to the ambulance on a stretcher and work on them on their way to the hospital.

▲ Inside an ambulance, everything is designed so that the crew can reach it easily.

Controls at the side of the fire engine can be used to raise and lower the ladder.

Quiz Corner

● Why do police cars have sirens and flashing lights?

● Why are emergency trucks always brightly colored?

● What can you find inside an ambulance?

19

look at: Cars, page 10; In the Future, page 28

Roads

A road is a strip of land that **vehicles** travel along. Thousands of years ago, long before cars were invented, the Romans began building roads. Carts traveled along these early roads, taking goods and people from one place to another. Today, roads cross most countries.

Road systems

Every town has roads that are connected to one another in a road system. **Engineers** plan the road system carefully to make sure the traffic flows smoothly.

▼ Large cities are linked by highways. These are big roads with a number of lanes. Cars can travel at high speeds on highways.

Building a road

Modern roads are built in stages. First, the **route** is chosen. Then soil and rocks are moved away to make the ground flat. Next, the ground is packed down to make it firm, then it is covered with layers of gravel, concrete and steel mesh. Finally another layer of concrete or asphalt is put on top.

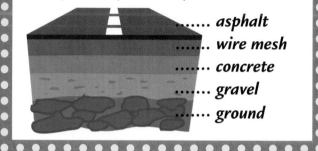

.... *asphalt*
.... *wire mesh*
.... *concrete*
.... *gravel*
.... *ground*

To get to a highway, cars must travel along a ramp.

An overpass is a road that is built above another road to let cars pass quickly, without stopping.

Instead of driving over or around mountains, cars can travel through tunnels to make journeys quicker.

Steep roads on mountainsides have sharp, or hairpin, curves make the climb less steep.

Bridges let cars cross rivers and deep valleys.

Drivers who do not want to visit the city center can use a bypass to travel around the edge of the city.

Quiz Corner

- What is an overpass?
- How do you get onto a highway?
- What are the stages in building a road?
- Who were one of the first people to build roads?

look at: Subway Trains, page 24

Trains

A train is a long line of cars that carries people or goods. An **engine** pulls or pushes the train along a track. The first trains were powered by steam, but today they are usually powered by **diesel** fuel or electricity. In 1825, the first steam railroad opened in England. In those days, trains were slow and bumpy. Today, trains are usually much faster.

Keeping on track
A train has special wheels that help it stay on the track. A lip, called a *flange*, sticks out from the inside edge of the wheel and keeps the train from sliding off the track.

flange

track

Modern trains
People are always trying to make better trains. Monorails run above the ground on a single rail. They are faster and cheaper to run than other trains. They are also much quieter because they have rubber wheels.

▼ Most monorails, such as this one in Sydney, Australia, are powered by electricity.

22

Quiz Corner

- Were the first trains powered by electricity or by steam?
- Why is the Rocket famous?
- Which kind of train carries goods?
- Which kind of train travels on a single rail?

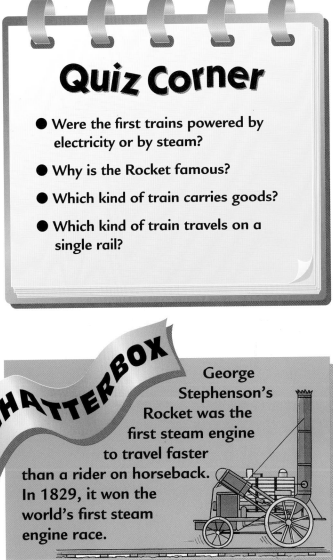

CHATTERBOX

George Stephenson's Rocket was the first steam engine to travel faster than a rider on horseback. In 1829, it won the world's first steam engine race.

Different kinds of trains

Freight trains carry goods and passenger trains carry people. A freight train can have up to 200 cars and is longer than a passenger train.

▼ Freight trains transport goods on land quickly. Only airplanes can travel faster.

23

look at: Buses and Trolleys, page 12; Trains, page 22

Subway Trains

Many cities have subways. When the roads are busy, it is usually quicker and easier to travel below ground. Subway trains carry many passengers at one time. They cause little **pollution** and they help to reduce traffic jams.

CHATTERBOX

When the subway in London, England, first opened, it used steam-powered trains. The smoke from the trains often made it impossible to see in the tunnels!

Subways around the world
The world's oldest and longest subway is in London. It opened in 1863. The subway with the most stations is in New York City, where there are 452 stops to travel between.

Tickets or tokens can be bought from a machine or ticket seller.

Automatic gates open when you put your ticket or token in the slot.

Moving staircases, called escalators, take you to the platforms.

Staff in the control room watch the trains and the platforms on video screens.

Emergency stairs can be used if the escalators break down.

Large maps on the walls help you plan your journey.

▼ **Beneath busy city streets, subways help keep people moving.**

Rush hour

Twice a day, in cities all over the world, thousands of people travel to and from work. This is called the rush hour and is the busiest time on the subway.

▲ **In Tokyo, Japan, the rush hour is so busy that people called shovers try to push more passengers into each car.**

The Channel Tunnel

Not all underground trains run under cities. The Channel Tunnel in Europe, which links England to France, runs under the sea. It was opened in 1994 and is about thirty miles long.

Quiz Corner

- Where is the world's oldest and longest subway system?

- What is the name of the tunnel between England and France?

- What are shovers, and where do they work?

look at: Animal Power, page 4

Traveling over Snow

In very cold northern areas, such as Lapland and Alaska, the ground is usually covered with ice and snow. This makes it difficult for people to travel by car. Instead, they use **vehicles** that are specially designed to travel over snowy or icy ground.

Traveling over snow and ice
In the past, sleds carried people and goods across icy, northern lands. The sleds were pulled by teams of huskies. Today, people usually prefer to travel in snowmobiles, which are powered by **engines**.

SEE FOR YOURSELF

Snowshoes are wider and flatter than ordinary shoes. This stops them from sinking into the snow. Try this test for yourself. Cut out a large shoe shape from cardboard and tie it to your foot. Keep your other foot bare and then walk across some sand. Which foot sinks?

▼ This sled driver is shouting instructions to his dogs. The number of dogs pulling the sled depends on the load.

▲ A snowmobile moves along on a belt and two skis, which steer it over icy ground.

Cross-country skiing

In snowy countries, such as Denmark, Norway and Finland, cross-country skiing is one of the cheapest and quickest ways to travel. It also keeps people in shape. At the winter Olympics, there are ski-jumping, cross-country and downhill competitions.

▲ Skiing can be an exciting winter sport.

Quiz Corner

- What kind of transportation do people often use today to travel across icy lands?

- Why is skiing a good way of traveling in some countries?

- Why are snowshoes wider than ordinary shoes?

look at: Cars, page 10; Buses and Trolleys, page 12

In the Future

Cars, buses, trucks and trains are always being improved to make traveling faster, safer and more comfortable. Fumes from **engines** can harm the **environment**, so it is important to use public transportation whenever possible, which saves **fuel** and reduces **pollution**.

Energy of the future

Many people are developing new types of transportation that use different kinds of **energy**, including electricity. Solar-powered cars take their energy from the light of the sun.

▶ **Special panels on this car turn energy from the sun into power.**

▲ **This car, designed in France, saves fuel by traveling great distances on a small amount of gasoline.**

Keeping things moving

New traffic control systems are being designed to help keep **vehicles** moving on busy roads. Cameras and computers can let traffic police know about problems such as traffic jams and accidents so that they can quickly go to help.

Quiz Corner

- From where do solar-powered cars take their energy?

- Why is it important to use public transportation?

- Why are navigational computers useful for drivers?

▲ A navigational computer in the front of a car can tell a driver the best **route** to take and warn of traffic jams ahead.

What next?

All the time, scientists are busy designing different vehicles to carry people and goods. These new types of transportation might look strange now, but soon you might see them in towns and cities everywhere.

▶ This tiny car fits inside a special suitcase. When it is not being driven, it can be folded away and carried.

Amazing Facts

● Did you know that there is a car that can fit into small parking spaces by scrunching up its back wheels? The Mantra Zoom, built by Renault, is still in its early stages and is not on the roads at the moment.

☆ The power of an engine is measured in units called horsepower. This is because the power of an engine is compared to the pulling power of a horse — so a one-horsepower engine is as powerful as one horse.

● Huskies really need their thick coats to keep them warm. At night, these dogs do not sleep in kennels but dig themselves beds in the snow.

☆ In Italy, there is a train that has been specially designed to lean inward when it goes around corners. This means that the train does not have to slow down as much for curves, making journeys faster.

● The largest train station in the world is Grand Central Station in New York City. It is built on two levels with forty-one tracks on the upper level and twenty-six on the lower level.

☆ An American named Henry Ford was the first car manufacturer to build cars on an assembly line. Here, ready-made parts for each car are fitted together at different places along a moving line. Each mechanic has to do just one job, so the cars can be built very quickly.

● The world's longest car is a twenty-six wheeled limousine, built in California. It is one hundred feet long and has an enormous water bed and a swimming pool in the back.

☆ Mexico City has some of the world's worst traffic jams. It also has over 60,000 taxis, which is more than any other city in the world.

Glossary

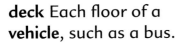

deck Each floor of a **vehicle**, such as a bus.

diesel A type of fuel used in some **engines**.

energy What gives living things or machines the **power** to do a job, such as to make an **engine** go.

engine A machine that changes **energy** into motion.

engineer Someone who designs things that are useful to people.

environment The world around us.

freight Goods moved from place to place by train, truck or ship.

friction The force caused by two surfaces rubbing together. When tires rub against a road surface, friction slows the wheels.

fuel Any substance that is burned to make heat or **energy**. **Engines** need fuel to make them work.

gear A device that changes the speed at which the wheels of a **vehicle** turn when the same amount of **energy** is being used.

pollute To spoil air, soil or water with garbage or other harmful things.

pollution Waste and unhealthy things dumped into the **environment**.

power The strength to do a job.

route The way you take to travel to a particular place.

siren A machine which makes a warning sound on an emergency **vehicle.**

spokes Thin bars that join the center, or hub, of a wheel to its outside, or rim.

streamlined Having a shape that lets air or water flow easily over it. A race car is streamlined to reduce air **friction**, making it as fast as possible.

tread The bumpy pattern on a tire, that helps the wheel to get a good grip on the road. The tread also pushes water away, making tires less likely to slip on wet roads.

vehicle Something used to carry people or goods from one place to another.

Index

Published in the USA by
C.D. Stampley Enterprises, Inc.,
Charlotte, NC, USA.
Created by Two-Can Publishing Ltd.,
London. English language edition
©Two-Can Publishing Ltd, 1997

Text: Deborah Chancellor
Consultant: Eryl Davies
Watercolour artwork: Colin King,
Stuart Trotter
Computer artwork: D Oliver

Editorial Director: Jane Wilsher
Art Director: Carole Orbell
Production Director: Lorraine Estelle
Project Manager: Eljay Yildirim
Editors: Belinda Webber,
Deborah Kespert
Assistant Editors: Julia Hillyard,
Claire Yude
Co-edition Editor: Leila Peerun
Photo Research:
Dipika Palmer-Jenkins

ISBN 0-915741-80-6

Photographic credits: Britstock-
IFA p15tr, p27tl; Colorific p26bl;
Hutchison Library (H.R. Dorig)
p4tr; Image Bank p14bl, p17tl,
p19tr; A.C. Press p29br;
Quadrant p14bc; Spectrum p5;
Tony Stone Images front cover,
p8b, p22-23c, p25tr; Frank
Spooner p28b&t, p29tl; Telegraph
Colour Library p18bl; Zefa p6bl,
p7cr, p9, p11t, p12, p26-27bc.